C000049342

The Observers Series
TRUCKS

About the Book

The New Observer's Book of Trucks is a completely new volume in the series and it surveys highway vehicles and special types of vehicle from all of the world's principal producers. The products of well over a hundred firms are covered, ranging from on- and off-road vehicles with engines from 100 bhp to 2,000 bhp and payload capabilities of a few to hundreds of tons. These standard highway haulage trucks are presented in a complete major section, but there are other sections which include details of vehicles built for special requirements—fire fighters, dump trucks, crane trucks, heavy haulage outfits and many more.

Like its related predecessor (*The Observer's Book of Commercial Vehicles* which sold tens of thousands of copies in five editions), this new volume is as valuable to people in the transport industry as it is to outside enthusiasts and general readers.

About the Author

Nick Baldwin has been writing about and living with trucks for over twenty years. After working for the makers of the versatile Land-Rover he entered the transport publishing field and has worked for the magazines *Commercial Vehicles*, *Motor Transport* and *Old Motor*. He is currently historical consultant to the *Vintage Commercial Vehicle Magazine* and is a regular contributor to *Truck*.

As well as collecting photographs and literature concerning modern and historic trucks, he has a small collection of old vehicles.

The *Observer's* series was launched in 1937 with the publication of *The Observer's Book of Birds*. Today, over fifty years later, paperback *Observers* continue to offer practical, useful information on a wide range of subjects, and with every book regularly revised by experts, the facts are right up-to-date. Students, amateur enthusiasts and professional organisations alike will find the latest *Observers* invaluable.

'Thick and glossy, briskly informative' – *The Guardian*

'If you are a serious spotter of any of the things the series deals with, the books must be indispensable' – *The Times Educational Supplement*

TRUCKS

Compiled by

Nick Baldwin

BLOOMSBURY BOOKS
LONDON

PENGUIN BOOKS

Published by the Penguin Group
Penguin Books Ltd, 27 Wrights Lane, London W8 5TZ, England
Penguin Books USA Inc., 375 Hudson Street, New York, New York 10014, USA
Penguin Books Australia Ltd, Ringwood, Victoria, Australia
Penguin Books Canada Ltd, 10 Alcorn Avenue, Toronto, Ontario, Canada M4V 3B2
Penguin Books (NZ) Ltd, 182–190 Wairau Road, Auckland 10, New Zealand

Penguin Books Ltd, Registered Offices: Harmondsworth, Middlesex, England

First published 1986

This edition published by Bloomsbury Books, an imprint of
The Godfrey Cave Group, 42 Bloomsbury Street, London, WC1B 3QJ,
under licence from Penguin Books Limited, 1993

1 3 5 7 9 10 8 6 4 2

ACKNOWLEDGEMENTS

My thanks go to all the manufacturers around the world who responded in time for this new edition. Some unfortunately sent catalogues or pictures that are difficult to reproduce, whilst others went to great lengths to provide us with exactly what we needed. As usual first prize for rapid response (perhaps rapid intervention would be appropriate in view of some of their products!) goes to Oshkosh. This is ironic as one of their chief rivals in America. FWD, has never yet managed to reply and unfortunately, has had to be delted from this edition.

In general, where no response was forthcoming, our 'spies on the ground' went into action to photograph elusive trucks. My grateful thanks go to the following overseas helpers: Vladimir Marsik and Margus Kuuse for covering the Comecon countries. Niels Jansen who lives in Holland, but has contacts in many other countries. Elliott Kahn in the USA and Nick Georgano, who lives in the Channel Islands and is a mine of information about worldwide vehicles of every sort. My thanks also to *Special Transport Magazine, PB 6146. NL-7401 J. C. Deventer, Holland, which is the only magazine concentrating exclusively on heavy haulage and cranes. Truck* magazine from FF Publishing, 97 Earls Court Road, London W8 6QH has also been most helpful.

Printed and bound in Great Britain by
BPCC Hazell Books Ltd

Member of BPCC Ltd

ISBN 1 85471 164 4

CONTENTS

INTRODUCTION

Unlike its related predecessor, *The Observer's Book of Commercial Vehicles*, this volume is concerned solely with trucks. This change allows far more scope to cover the major groups producing trucks and leaves room later in the book to look at the many specialist makers and the multifarious tasks undertaken by custom-built chassis.

The worldwide truck industry has contracted since the last edition in 1981 and several firms have ceased production. Others have embarked on complex technical or commercial liaisons with former rivals. These are outlined where possible in the major make headings. The explanation for this trend is that with falling output it is often difficult for one manufacturer to recover the cost of developing one truck, let alone a whole new range. An example is Mack, which has never been strong in the mid-weight range and now imports Renault components to enable it to compete successfully. Numerous Japanese firms provide vehicles to European and American manufacturers to complete their ranges. Another way of economizing is to buy in proprietary components from specialists. Gearboxes, axles and engines from firms able to spread their production costs over several truck-making customers are now commonplace. Indeed, in America virtually all heavy trucks can be built from the same kit of mechanical parts, though the skill comes in selecting the best combinations for particular transport duties. For example, unladen weight and therefore maximum payload may be critical for some operations—or durability or longevity or speed or a combination of these attributes.

To obtain the maximum space for showing trucks, we have cut back on the headings for particular makes. This means that the potted histories of each firm cannot be included. Fortunately this interesting topic is receiving increasingly wide coverage in such specialist magazines as *Truck* and *The Automobile* published respectively by FF and PPG in London, and in *The Vintage Commercial*

Vehicle magazine from Axbridge in Somerset. There are also several useful books including the *Complete Encyclopaedia of Commercial Vehicles* edited by G. N. Georgano, and a forthcoming Dictionary on the background history of individual motor manufacturers being published by Orbis, to which Nick Baldwin has contributed.

Abbreviations and glossary

artic = articulated
bhp = brake horse power (quoted net installed where possible)
bonnet = hood (US)
forward control = cab over (US) i.e. engine under cab
GCW = gross combined weight (tractive unit and semi trailer)
GTW = gross train weight (tractor and trailer(s))
GVW = gross vehicle weight
normal control = conventional (US)
synchro = synchromesh easy-change gearbox
tilt-cab = cab hinges forward for engine access
turbo = turbocharged engine induction
V-6, V-8, etc = six or eight cylinders in vee formation (i.e.) a V-6 has two banks of three cylinders. Where simply six cylinders are mentioned the engine is an in-line unit
4 × 2, 4 × 4, 6 × 6, etc. = number of wheels (double tyres count as one) × number driven by engine, i.e. 8 × 4 has 8 wheels (four axles) and 4 driven wheels (two axles)
tonnes = metric tonnes (1,000 kgs)
tons = either 2,240 lbs British or 2,000 lbs American short

ENGINES AND PROPRIETARY COMPONENTS

Very few of the world's heavy truck making groups rely exclusively on their own engines. There are exceptions like MAN and Scania, but at the other end of the scale comes the equally famous PACCAR which makes Peterbilt, Kenworth and Foden trucks yet builds none of its own engines.

In between come other big names like Leyland, Mack and Navistar International who make engines in some power ranges and also offer proprietary units.

A few truck firms build virtually all their own components, but even so are not averse to including alternative specifications in some markets. Thus some Mercedes-Benz trucks have ZF gearboxes and some DAFs have Rockwell axles.

Many of the great transmission and engine specialists are North American in origin or ownership, like Cummins, Caterpillar, Detroit (unusual in being a proprietary engine firm owned by a major truck maker—GMC, which also runs Allison transmissions), Perkins (primarily British based but partly Canadian owned and the proprietors of Rolls-Royce diesels since 1983), Dana-Spicer, Rockwell and Timken. These firms all have overseas manufacturing plants and Britain is an important centre for them. This is highlighted by the use of the plants of three former vehicle makers (Turner, Thornycroft and Maudslay) by American owners to make transmissions. Very important in the engine field is Cummins, which has made engines in Britain since 1956.

There are also major indigenous European producers like the British GKN Group (which includes Kirkstall axles and Hardy Spicer), the German ZF concern and many more, like axle makers Heathfield, Soma and Kessler.

In addition to the proprietary engine makers already mentioned Britain has the respected Gardner diesel engine firm now owned by Hawker-Siddeley, Germany has MWM and Deutz, both of whom are unusual in offering air-cooled diesels. Deutz was until recently the parent of Magirus, now one of the truck making con-stituents of the IVECO group. Italy has the co-operative Sofim diesel engine plant as well as VM making pro-prietary commercial vehicle diesels. In South Africa a plan to make a national heavy truck diesel with help from Mercedes-Benz has resulted in the Atlantis engine.

So, a heavy truck brought in America or Britain is likely to have many familiar transmission components and a choice of engines by Cummins, Caterpillar or Detroit in the USA, and in Britain by Cummins, Gardner or Perkins (Rolls-Royce) diesels.

The other European makers, at home at least, will have mostly their own components though specialists including the major ones like MOL, Kaelble and Faun use bought-in components and engines. As well as mechanical components, several firms use other people's cabs or cab designs—so Foden or FTF may look similar because of their Motor Panels cabs, Mercedes-Benz styling is found on FAP and Titan, DAF on AVM, Irtex and others, MAN on numerous Comecon types such as Roman and RABA (MAN also supplies much engine technology) and Volvo on Terberg. Not sur-prisingly fellow members of the same group share as many common items as possible. Thus some Scammells look like Leylands and Ivecos appear the same whether by Fiat or Magirus.

Since the last edition of the *Observer's Book of Com-mercial Vehicles* the trend towards the gradual dis-appearance of petrol engines in trucks has continued, though Russia and America still favour mid-weight pet-rol engined trucks. Turbocharged diesels have spread into most weight ranges instead of just the highest power categories. Turbocharging is the name given to a method of boosting the pressure of the fuel/air mixture injected into the combustion chamber using exhaust gases to drive the turbo, that can be likened to a pump. This greatly increases the efficiency of an engine designed specifically to withstand the pressure of being turbocharged and is further improved by charge-cooling or intercooling of the mixture before it is injected. Normally aspirated engines (as non-turbo types are known) generally require greater overall size and swept volume for a given power output than their turbo sisters. An example is the typical 14 litre Cummins diesel (sometimes lightly turbocharged) that powered many top weight highway trucks in the 1970s. In its place many similar trucks are now powered by 10 litre Cummins turbo diesels, and Volvo and Scania in particular are great believers in even smaller turbo engines giving high bhp outputs. Some operators maintain that a lightly stressed, larger engine lasts longest. Against this must be weighed the loss of payload sacrificed with a heavier engine, that is anyway likely to produce more torque and therefore require a more robust and heavier transmission. Protagonists of vee formation and in-line engines are equally divided, the main advantage of the former configuration being compact dimensions for the number of cylinders involved and parts interchangeability over a number of different engines, as for example in the Detroit V-4, V-6, V-8, V-12 family. Just as Deutz and Tatra are relatively unusual with their air-cooling, so Detroit is unconventional in another way with its adherence to the two-stroke cycle. Two-stroke engines have less moving parts than four-strokes and work at higher speeds so can use smaller and lighter components for a given power output. They are at the most efficient working hard at near constant revs.

Space permits only one final observation about components and that is the increasing adoption of synchro and automatic gearboxes, even on heavy trucks. Many experienced drivers brought up on constant mesh or even sliding mesh crash gearboxes do not like the 'feel' of synchro or lack of control of an automatic. These gearboxes are also more costly, are heavier and have more parts to go wrong. However, it seems likely that both will increase, particularly for short-haul or urban duties, before the next edition of the *New Observer's Book of Trucks*.

MAJOR GROUPS

Comecon

Truck manufacture takes a high priority in the Eastern
Bloc countries and is organized on national as opposed
to company lines. Many of the vehicles use component
designs built under licence from Western manufacturers.
In Russia various individual factories specialize in separate models and this applies to several other countries.
For example, Liaz in Czechoslovakia makes on-highway
trucks and Tatra concentrates on cross-country and special purpose vehicles. A random selection is shown here
of the types most likely to be encountered in the West.

This Czech **Liaz** has an 11·69 litre six-cylinder diesel
and is part of an extensive range produced by a factory
associated with the makers of Avia and Skoda light
vehicles. Some of their products are sold abroad by
Motokov. Some Liaz vehicles are made in Bulgaria
under the name Madara.

Tatra T815 is a 6 × 6 chassis for many purposes with V-8, V-10 or V-12 air-cooled diesels of up to 320 bhp. GVW of this example is 26·6 tonnes. It has a central backbone chassis and swing axle suspension. Components from it are used in the West German Semex.

The Yugoslavian **FAP 2626BK** 6 × 4 tipper uses a Mercedes-Benz-licence built cab and 11 litre six-cylinder diesel and six-speed synchromesh gearbox. GVW is 26 tonnes. Lighter vehicles are built in Yugoslavia by Zastava under Fiat licence.

Built with the help of American, British and French technology since 1978 is the Russian **Kamaz** range. The latest types have V-8 260 bhp air-cooled diesels. They have tilt cabs and power steering.

Czechoslovakian **Avia A30** has a 3·6 litre, four-cylinder diesel, four-speed synchromesh gearbox and is for 6 tonnes GVW. It has a fixed steel cab and coil sprung front axle with conventional leaf springs at the rear.

Known by the nickname Crocodile in Russia because of its appearance is the **ZIL GJA.** This 6 × 4 example has a V-8 210 bhp diesel.

Kraz 256 replaced the earlier Diamond T based model in the early 1980s and now has a V-8 300 bhp four-stroke diesel. Early types had two-stroke engines. This 6 × 4 example is for sixteen-tonne loads.

The first Russian transcontinental 38 tonne truck is the
MAZ 6422. It has a turbo V-8 14·86 litre 320 bhp diesel
with eight-speed gearbox and a steel tilt-cab.

GAZ 53A is one of numerous bonneted 4 × 2 models
produced in Russia, often with petrol engines. This one
has a 7 m³ compression refuse body and has a GVW of
7·1 tonnes.

The Hungarian **RABA** is made by a firm that produces axles for several European manufacturers. Its trucks use much MAN technology, this F22.188–6.2 having a 256 bhp six-cylinder turbo diesel, Csepel synchro gearbox and ZF power steering. It has a liftable third axle and is for 22·5 tonnes GVW or 38 tonnes GCW.

Like RABA, **Roman** of Romania use MAN cabs and components. This is its **19.215 DFK** 6 × 4 215 bhp tipper assembled under licence in Yugoslavia. Also using MAN type cabs in Romania is DAC, which in addition makes heavy dumpers plus normal control trucks of Russian appearance.

Polish light commercials include Nysa and Zuk whilst its heavy trucks are by Star or Jelcz. This is a six-tonne capacity **Star 200** with 150 bhp diesel and tilt cab developed in conjunction with Chausson in France.

TAM vehicles made in Yugoslavia owe their technical origins to Magirus in its pre-IVECO days. This **T11 BK** 5·5 tonne capacity tipper has an air-cooled 128 bhp diesel and ZF hydraulic gearbox.

A pair of Yugoslavian Zastava light trucks showing their obvious Fiat/IVECO origins. On the left is a **645AD** and on the right a **642N.**

The IFA made in East Germany was formerly known as the Robur and before that the Phanomen. This **W-50** has a MAN licence, four-cylinder, 125 bhp diesel with five-speed synchro gearbox, and is shown here with road sweeping suction equipment powered by a separate 50 bhp diesel. GVW is 10·8 tonnes.

The **Madara 452** made in Bulgaria is basically a Russian Gaz 53A built under licence but instead of the petrol engine of the original it has a Perkins diesel.

The Polish **Jelcz W640JS** is for 17·5 tonne loads and has a six-cylinder 11·1 litre 240 bhp turbo diesel built under licence from Leyland, axles of Steyr type and a ZF six-speed synchro splitter gearbox.

DAF

DAF, makes about 15,000 commercial vehicles per year and employs 8,700 people worldwide. Cabs and axles are made in Belgium and engine manufacture and assembly takes place in Holland. DAF has a joint cab project with ENASA. International had an important stake in the firm until 1983. DAF has assembly plants in Portugal, Morocco, Zimbabwe (where AVM uses DAF components), Ivory Coast and Australia (where it operates the old White Western Star factory). In 1986 it began to market some lighter Leyland models under its own name.

N2800 normal control models are primarily for export and have DAF 11·6 litre diesels rated at 230 to 330 bhp. There is an eight-speed synchro gearbox with splitter option on each ratio. GTW of up to 140 tonnes is available.

DAF military vehicles are made at Geldrop, Holland and include 4 × 4 and 6 × 6 trucks and armoured vehicles. Most use versions of the 11·6 litre diesel which owes its origins to a Leyland design.

DAF **330** turbo intercooled 330 bhp 6 × 6 articulated outfit built to Middle Eastern specification. Rigid versions are available with two, three and four axles.

DAF **1800** 4 × 4 has an 8·25 litre 156 bhp naturally aspirated engine. Its 4 × 2 1600 sister has 6·15 litre diesels rated at 115 to 151 bhp.

From the 2300 series we see a **FAG 2305** with second steering axle. It has an 8·25 litre turbo diesel and six-speed synchro gearbox with splitter gear to give twelve ratios.

Dodge

Dodge in America is part of the Chrysler Corp. It had numerous overseas factories making trucks, notably in Spain and Britain, but these were sold in the late 1970s to Peugeot-Citroen and are now listed under Renault. Chrysler has a 14 per cent stake in the Peugeot-Citroen business and owns 15 per cent of Mitsubishi Motors in Japan, from whom it buys many engines and complete vehicles.

Dodge no longer makes heavy trucks and for 1986 its largest model was for 5·5 tons GVW. Shown is a **W150 Royal SE Ram** pickup for 3·2 tons GVW. Manual or automatic gearboxes are available with 3·7, 5·2 and 5·9 litre petrol engines.

ENASA

ENASA is the Spanish government-controlled heavy commercial vehicle company that makes Pegaso vehicles. Until 1978 it was partly owned by International Harvester and, through them, was linked to DAF and Seddon Atkinson. In 1983 ENASA acquired Seddon Atkinson and also has a joint firm with DAF to produce truck cabs. ENASA's lighter SAVA vans are based on designs from Leyland, as indeed are its heavy truck engines. The Seddon Atkinson name is the result of the merger of these two successful British trucks firms in 1970.

Pegaso makes two-, three- and four-axle forward control tilt cab trucks in its new Tecno range. This is its turbo intercooled **1234T** with 340 bhp diesel and sixteen-spread ZF gearbox. GVW is 38 tonnes.

British Seddon Atkinson **201** has International Harvester or Perkins six-cylinder diesels of 134 or 149 bhp and an Eaton synchro five-speed gearbox. Special versions are offered for stop-start municipal use with ZF or Allison gearboxes. The tilt-cab is basically steel with plastics front apron and wings. GVW is 16·27 tonnes.

Seddon Atkinson **401** 38 tonne outfit with second steering axle. It can have Cummins, Rolls-Royce or Gardner diesels of 288 to 328 bhp with Fuller nine-speed gearbox. Various two-, three- and four-axle maximum capacity trucks are offered in the 301/401 series.

Ford

Ford is one of the world's major truck producers. In Louisville, USA it has the largest single truck factory in the West and it has a major operation in Britain. Other factories produce Ford vehicles as far afield as Brazil, the Philippines, South Africa and Turkey. Its Cargo range was introduced in 1981, whilst its well-known Transit first appeared twenty years ago. Ford owns an important minority stake in the Japanese makers of Mazda trucks and markets some with Ford badges. As we closed for press Ford (Britain) and IVECO merged their heavy truck operations

The **Transit** has petrol or diesel engines of 65 to 100 bhp and is available for GVW up to 3·5 tonnes. They can have manual or automatic transmissions and a wide assortment of bodywork.

The Cargo is made in several forms around the world, including one with a fibreglass cab in Turkey and as a 'world truck' in Brazil with 110–225 bhp diesels. This is a British **0813** for 7·5 tonnes GVW. It has a six-cylinder 6·2 litre 131 bhp Ford diesel.

The higher powered Cargos in Europe have Ford, Perkins, Cummins or Deutz diesels. The 6 × 4 typically has an engine of about 200 bhp. A Hendrickson two-spring tandem is available and there can be single or double drive.

27

In North America Ford makes an extensive range of cab over and conventional trucks. This example is an **LTL 9000,** which can have various Cummins, Detroit and Caterpillar engines of up to 435 bhp and 8-, 9-, 10-, 13- or 15-ratio gearboxes. Maximum GTW is 77 tons and GVW 30 tons.

Mazda T3000 is produced in Japan by a firm in which Ford holds a 33 per cent stake. It has four-cylinder 2-litre petrol or 2·5- or 3-litre diesel engines of 65 to 76 bhp and five-speed synchro gearbox versions from 3·5 to 6 tonnes GVW are offered.

The aluminium cab-over heavy-duty American Fords include the **CLT-9000** for up to 62·6 tonnes GCW. Cummins, Detroit or Caterpillar diesels of up to 600 bhp are available with the usual Spicer or Fuller transmission options and Rockwell drive axles.

American **Ford F-700** conventional range includes six-cylinder and V-8 petrol engined models of 164 to 213 bhp. GVW of this one is 12·5 tons or up to 30 tons with trailer.

GMC

The American based General Motors Corporation owns or has financial interests in numerous truck producers around the world. Its most famous commercial vehicle brand names include Chevrolet and GMC in America, Bedford in Britain, Opel in Germany, Dina in Mexico and engine/transmission makers Detroit/Allison. GM holds minority interests in the Japanese firms Isuzu and Suzuki. GMC makes Titan and Terex dumptrucks (see Construction Industry Trucks section).

Chevrolet makes light and medium weight trucks, many of which are also available with GMC badging. This is a conventional **C60** available with petrol engines or 160 bhp diesels by Detroit or Caterpillar. Articulated GCW is 22·5 tons and manual or automatic transmission is offered.

Available as a GMC Forward or Chevy Tiltmaster is this
Isuzu built 15 tons GVW cab-over. Power comes from
an Isuzu 5·8 litre 165 bhp six-cylinder turbo diesel.

The **GMC Brigadier** range covers two- and three-axle
rigids and artics. Various diesels by Cummins, Caterpillar
and Detroit are offered between 166 and 348 bhp. The
steel cab has a fibreglass bonnet.

The **GMC General** is available for GCW of up to 65 tons and GVW of 40 tons. Detroit, Cummins and Caterpillar diesels ranging from 268 bhp to 468 bhp are offered. Manual transmissions with up to 15 forward ratios are available. The cab is of aluminium construction.

GMC Astro cab-over can have Detroit or Cummins diesels of 294 to 468 bhp and aluminium tilt cab with sleeping compartment. This example is for 45 tons GCW and has a 400 bhp Detroit diesel.

The **Bedford** range starts with numerous vans and pick-ups outside our weight limit. The largest of them, the CF2, shown here in double rear wheel form, goes up to 3·5 tonnes GVW. It has 2 litre petrol or 2·3 litre diesel engines of 78 bhp or 61 bhp respectively. GM Four or ZF five-speed gearboxes are specified and some mid-range versions have front disc brakes.

Bedford TL range covers tilt cab models of 5·7 to 24·4 tonnes GVW plus artics and drawbar units. This is the smallest TL 570 with 3·6 litre 90 bhp turbo diesel and four-speed synchro gearbox.

33

The largest of the **TL** range is the **TL 2440** with 8·2 litre turbo Bedford 210 bhp diesel. This is a 6 × 4 with Whale gulley cleaning equipment. Six- or nine-speed gearboxes are available.

The **TM** comes as two- or three-axle rigids and artics. This is an extra heavy duty version built for Middle Eastern operation at 60 tonnes GCW. It has a 312 bhp Detroit turbo diesel and Fuller nine-speed gearbox.

Dina's vehicles still show signs of their International and Diamond-Reo origins. However, all have been built under the control of GM since 1985. This is a **661-G2** with Cummins 210 bhp V-8 diesel and five-speed Spicer synchro gearbox plus two-speed Eaton drive axle. GVW is 20·9 tonnes.

Dina 861-K1 is for 41 tonnes GCW and has a Cummins six-cylinder 350 bhp diesel and Spicer 14-ratio gearbox. It has Rockwell axles and air brakes.

Having shown a GMC badged **Isuzu** we now have a true Japanese version. This is a basic 6 × 6 TW model for 14 tonnes GVW. It has a five-speed synchro gearbox with two-speed transfer box and is powered by a 150 bhp 5·8 litre six-cylinder diesel.

Isuzu EXZ can have 258 to 384 bhp diesels and Isuzu six-speed or Fuller nine- or thirteen-speed gearboxes. GCW, depending on specification, is 41 to 50 tonnes.

International

International is America's largest producer of trucks of over 7 tons GVW. It was part of a major agricultural engineering empire that was split up into numerous separate companies in the 1980s, following the financial difficulties that afflicted the motor industry. In 1986 the truck-making firm became Navistar International though its vehicles are still called Internationals. Its interests in several other truck firms like ENASA, DAF, Seddon-Atkinson, Pacific and also International Pay-hauler dumptrucks were sold. The International firm in Australia sells about a quarter of the trucks in its weight range and has links with Nissan. It markets Nissans as Internationals and also retains the Atkinson name on some heavy models.

American-built International **9370** 6 × 4 conventional available with usual proprietary engine and transmission options. This one for 70 tons GCW has numerous aluminium components to save weight, including wheels and tanks and has a Detroit 400 bhp diesel.

The **XL** series of American cab overs can have Detroit or Cummins diesels from 270 to 475 bhp and 7–15 ratio manual or 4–5 ratio automatic gearboxes. Some have compressed air engine starters.

Paystar 5000 series made in America can be of 4 × 2, 4 × 4, 6 × 4, 6 × 6, 8 × 4 or 8 × 6 configuration and is for rugged work. Cummins or Detroit diesels run up to 445 bhp and there are 5–15 speed transmissions.

The S series is made in both America and Australia. This
S-2600 operates in Australia (note the 'roo bar') and is
part of a range of 4 × 2 and 6 × 4 models for GCW of up
to 54 tonnes. The fibreglass bonnet houses International
or Cummins diesels.

ACCO is the name for Australian Constructed Cab Over
and is shown here in 6 × 4 **ACCO-C** tipper form. It has
fully bolted chassis construction and Cummins 190 bhp
diesel. Other versions can have Perkins or International
diesels.

ACCO T-2600 series covers 4 × 2, 6 × 4 and 8 × 4 models with International or Cummins diesels. GVW is up to 26·5 tonnes and GCW up to 54 tonnes.

Australian **Atkinson F4870** now uses a version of the ACCO tilt cab. Cummins or Detroit diesels of 300 to 407 bhp come with 14 transmission and 11 axle options.

IVECO

IVECO

Fiat is the dominant partner in the Industrial Vehicles Corporation formed in 1975. Fiat had earlier taken over most of its Italian rivals followed by Unic in France in 1969. In 1975 Magirus-Deutz and Fiat created IVECO and from mid-1983 all the group's vehicles were badged IVECO. Most of the Deutz interests in IVECO were bought out, leaving the German firm freer to supply other vehicle makers. Nowadays the Unic's contribution to IVECO is limited to buses and engines in the 200 to 300 bhp range. As we closed for press, Ford (Britain) and IVECO merged their heavy truck operations.

Turbo Grinta for 3·5 tonnes GVW has an 80 bhp diesel. Of similar appearance is the Ducato van built jointly with Talbot, Alfa-Romeo and others.

IVECO Z range covers numerous trucks in the 5 to 11 tonne range. This is a 79.14 model for 8·1 tonnes GVW with 135 bhp diesel. It has a non-tilting cab.

From the medium range comes this **135.17** for 13·3 tonnes GVW. Its six-cylinder diesel develops 168 bhp and it has a tilt-cab. Broadly similar cabs are used on all IVECO's forward control models above 11 tonnes GVW.

Flagship of the international haulage IVECO range is the **Turbo Star** with high specification sleeper cab and wind deflector. This 190.42 has a 420 bhp Fiat diesel and is for 40 ton GCW or 19 tonnes as a solid rigid.

Produced in the Magirus factory in Germany is a range of normal control two- and three-axle trucks, often with Deutz air-cooled diesels. This is a 6 × 4 **330.32** with 330 bhp Deutz engine and a GVW of 33 tonnes.

Leyland

Britain's largest maker of heavy trucks is Leyland. Over the years it has come to control at least a dozen other manufacturers. Since 1980 it has introduced completely new ranges. Nowadays its non-car derived van range is made by Freight-Rover (Land-Rover), and its specialist vehicles are produced by Scammell. Leyland has numerous overseas interests, including a minority shareholding in Ashok Leyland, one of India's principal truck makers, and in BMC Sanayi in Turkey. From 1986 the lighter DAFs are in fact Leylands.

Most recent of the **T45** range is the Roadrunner, launched in 1984. It uses Leyland 97 or 115 bhp diesels and is for 6·2 to 10 tonnes GVW. This example is a 7·5 tonne 8.12 with the larger engine and five-speed synchro gearbox. Note the low kerb spotting window.

The **Freighter** range covers 10·99 to 16·26 tonnes GVW trucks. They use Leyland engines of 115 to 180 bhp and are available with day or sleeper (shown) tilt-cabs. The same narrow T45 cab is also used on the Cruiser artic range with engines of 160 to 260 bhp.

A Leyland **Roadtrain** 4 × 2 with semi-trailer for 38 tonne GVW leads a 30 ton GVW **Constructor** 8 × 4. The Roadtrain uses Rolls-Royce or Cummins engines of 265 to 350 bhp whilst the Constructor built by Scammell has Leyland, Gardner, Cummins or Rolls-Royce engines of 160 to 265 bhp.

45

Amongst a large selection of special export trucks is the Leyland **Landmaster.** It uses the Leyland 698 diesel and is for GVW of 9 to 12 tonnes. Some well known forward control types like the Clydesdale and Boxer remain available for tough overseas conditions.

The **Landtrain** comes in two- and three-axle versions for solo or trailer operation. Cummins 250 or 290 bhp diesels are utilized. GVW is up to 36 tonnes and GTW to 65 tonnes. Here we see an articulated, double bottom outfit.

Amongst Scammell's specialist vehicles are airfield crash tenders, military vehicles and heavy haulage tractors. Here we have an **S26** 6 × 6 with Rolls-Royce 290 bhp turbo diesel and Fuller eight-speed gearbox. It is equipped for heavy recovery with a 15 tonne crane and 25 tonne winch and it can climb a 43% gradient.

S24 65 tonne capacity tank transporter has Cummins 350 bhp turbo diesel, Fuller fifteen-speed gearbox, 6 × 6 and 20 tonne winch. A larger Commander version is also offered with Rolls-Royce 625 bhp turbo diesel.

The **Freight-Rover Sherpa** range includes vans and light trucks of 2 to 3·5 tonnes GVW. This is a 350 dropside truck with 2 litre 84 bhp petrol or 2·5 litre 70 bhp diesel and five-speed synchro gearbox. Some versions became the first to use carbon fibre springs in 1985.

Ashok Leyland Comet produced in Madras has Leyland six-cylinder 6·1 litre 110 bhp diesel and five-speed constant mesh gearbox. It is for 12·2 tonnes GVW and has a fixed cab.

MAN

MAN is part of an important engineering complex owned by major German financial institutions. It currently makes about 20,000 heavy vehicles in Germany, of which 60 per cent are exported, and has various overseas involvements including Shakti-MAN in India and a factory in Turkey capable of about 5,000 trucks per year. It provides technical expertise to numerous other companies and has many Comecon links (e.g. RABA and Roman). MAN and VW introduced a joint mid range in 1979 and MAN controls ÖAF in Austria, which makes many of its specialized vehicles up to a 700 bhp 250 tonne tractive unit.

The **MAN-VW** joint range covers six to nine tonnes GVW. This example is for 3·5 tonne loads (7·49 tonnes GVW) and has a six-cylinder 5·69 litre 136 bhp diesel.

Various rugged traditional export models are produced like this **32.321** 6 × 6 logger. For 32 tonnes GVW it can handle GCW of up to 90 tonnes and has a 321 bhp diesel, though other versions span 240 to 360 bhp.

One of MAN's upper midweight range, which was formerly covered by MAN-VW types. Covering 12 to 16 tonnes they have 136 bhp six-cylinder diesels, which in turbo form give 170 to 192 bhp. This **12.170F** has a 6·5 tonne payload capacity and with trailer can gross 26 tonnes.

Amongst MAN's multi axle highway range is this 8 × 4
30 tonner. The four-axle models can have 240, 290, 330
or 360 bhp diesels and 8 × 4, 8 × 6 or 8 × 8. This is a
30.291 transit mixer.

As part of its all-wheel drive range, versions of the
MAN-VW are available with 4 × 4. This 8/9 tonne GVW
fire appliance has a 136 bhp diesel and five-speed synchro gearbox plus transfer box.

Mercedes-Benz

The world's largest producer of heavy trucks is Mercedes-Benz. Roughly 200,000 are sold each year and its parent company Daimler-Benz also controls NAW (the Swiss factories that formerly built Saurer and FBW trucks), Freightliner (acquired in 1981 in the split up of the old White firm) and Mevosa in Spain. It has close commercial and technical ties with the Austrian half-state-owned Steyr firm, and technical liaison with such factories as FAP (Comecon).

Two **Transporter** van and light truck ranges are offered which between them cover 2·5 to 6·79 tonnes GVW. Petrol engines are offered, though most are powered by four, five- or six-cylinder diesels developing up to 130 bhp. Most have five-speed synchro gearboxes though a four-speed torque converter type is available.

An extensive selection of 4 × 4 **Unimogs** are offered from about 50 to 200 bhp. They can be equipped with all manner of specialized equipment and bodywork. This 1700L is in use in the USA and has an armour plated body by Federal Motors, themselves the makers of various specialized chassis.

From the new midweight range we see a **1320** drawbar outfit. It has a 6 litre 201 bhp six-cylinder diesel and six-speed synchro gearbox. The same tilt-cab covers the 6·5 to 13 tonne range and is shown here in sleeper form. Twin circuit air braking is provided.

A **1638** shown with full factory specification aerodynamic equipment. GCW is 38 tonnes. Power comes from a turbo intercooled Mercedes V-8 375 bhp diesel with sixteen-speed ZF gearbox.

In production for many years, the L series of semi-forward control fixed cab no-frills models are especially popular in export markets. Two- and three-axle types are offered. This **L1113** is for 7·3 tonne loads and has 138 or 168 bhp six-cylinder diesels and five-speed synchro gearbox.

Six models of four-axle trucks are offered, many made in the Saurer plant in Switzerland. Three concrete mixer versions are available with 250 or 280 bhp diesels and power take-offs to drive the equipment.

The **3850A** is an all-wheel drive heavy duty tractor. Its GVW is 38 tonnes and it can handle GTW of up to 220 tonnes. It has a Mercedes V-10, 18·3 litre 500 bhp diesel and a sixteen-speed ZF gearbox with torque converter.

Freightliner in the Mercedes-Benz group make over 10,000 heavy trucks per year in the USA. Their standard aluminium cabbed **COE** model has Cummins 300 bhp diesels, Fuller nine-speed gearboxes and Rockwell axles but there are numerous alternative specifications.

Freightliner Conventional is for 40 tons GCW and has an aluminium cab shown here with sleeper pod. The standard engine is a 300 bhp Cummins with Fuller nine-speed gearbox and Rockwell axles. The steel chassis has aluminium crossmembers.

Freightliner Medium Conventional range can have set-forward or set-back front axle (former shown) and is for urban and inter-city use. Cummins engines of 270 to 350 bhp are optional with 7-, 9-, 10- or 13-speed gearboxes and single or double drive tandems. GCW is 40 tons. Chassis and cab are of all-steel construction.

Steyr in Austria has close links with Mercedes-Benz and produces the latter's G-Wagen 4 × 4 models. Steyr also make VW's 4 × 4 types and Fiat's light 4 × 4s. This is a **Steyr 1891.320** 8 × 4 tipper with 320 bhp twelve litre diesel. Steyr have recently won a major Chinese order and have sold a production licence to Jelcz (see Comecon).

Mitsubishi

Mitsubishi Motors of Tokyo has commercial and technical links with Chrysler (Dodge) and is 15 per cent owned by the American company. This means that Mitsubishi vehicles are sold in various parts of the world under the Dodge brand name. Mitsubishi's light trucks are known as Canters whilst heavy trucks are Fusos, although in recent years most carry the Mitsubishi name.

Mitsubishi makes a wide range of trucks, including some of the heaviest in Japan. Shown here is an 8 tonne GVW 154 bhp model. Examples of its heavy types can be found in the section on crane carriers and opposite.

Mitsubishi **NV113K** is a 6 × 4 chassis with V-8, 14·9 litre, 280 bhp diesel and six-speed gear box. Its GVW is 25·4 tonnes, of which 9·6 tonnes represent its unladen weight.

Mitsubishi **FV** is a forward control version of the NV with similar V-8 engine. The FV has 6 × 4 but a 6 × 2 FU is also built and the two types cover GVWs of 21·4 to 27·7 tonnes.

Nissan

This major Japanese group makes Nissan light commercials, Nissan UD heavy commercials and has controlled Ebro in Spain since 1980. Nissan has several plants around the world including one in Tennessee, USA, where planned output is 180,000 light commercials per year. Nissan UD employs 7,000 men in Japan whilst the Nissan Motor Co. employs 60,000, the majority of whom, however, are involved with its passenger cars.

Cabstar range from Nissan is for 3·4 to 5·9 tonnes GVW and includes this crewcab **Atlas** version for 4·1 tonnes GVW. Various petrol and diesel engines of up to 3·3 litres and 132 bhp are available. Some Nissans are sold in Australia as Internationals.

UD trucks from Nissan Diesel include the **CMA/CMD** range. This has six cylinder 5·65 litre diesels which develop 150 bhp or 177 bhp in turbo form. They are for 9·5 tonne GVW and have steel tilt-cabs.

Nissan Diesel **CWA** is a 6 × 4 tilt-cab chassis with 11·7 litre, 275 bhp six-cylinder turbo diesel and six- or nine-speed gearbox. GCW is up to 45 tonnes and GVW 25·5 tonnes or 24 tonnes off road.

Ebro Trade is made by Nissan in Spain. This is a 3·5 tonne GVW version with 2·82 litre four cylinder 68 bhp diesel and five-speed synchro gearbox.

An extensive range of forward control trucks of 4·5 to 12·5 tonnes GVW is offered by Ebro. These use Perkins engines of up to 5·8 litres and 129 bhp. A special Ebro for the distribution trade has a central backbone chassis.

PACCAR

PACCAR

This major premium truck group derives its title from Pacific Car and Foundry, a firm with longstanding transport engineering interests. It owns Peterbilt and Kenworth in North America, Kenmex in Mexico and acquired Foden in Britain in 1980. An Australian plant holds a local market share of about ten per cent of its weight category. Kenworth and Peterbilt each build over 10,000 trucks per year and use well known proprietary mechanical components in their construction. Peterbilts are produced in Newark, California, Madison, Tennessee and Denton, Texas whilst Kenworth's come from Bellvue, Washington, Akron, Ohio and Kansas City, Missouri, the latter specializing in cab overs.

Kenworth **T600A** is a highly aerodynamic unit offering up to 22 per cent improved fuel economy. Its standard engine is a Cummins 270 bhp diesel with various transmission options. GCW is 40 tons.

Kenworth **K100E** has aluminium and fibreglass cab with roof-mounted sleeper compartment. It can have most American proprietary engines in the 250 to 450 bhp band and numerous transmission options. GCW is 40 tons.

Both Kenworth and Peterbilt offer low cab overs for multi-stop work. This is an **L700** with Caterpillar, Cummins or Detroit diesels of 230 to 350 bhp and Fuller or Allison transmissions. Air suspension is available.

Peterbilt and Kenworth make numerous ultra-heavy duty models for on-off or off highway use, some of which are also assembled by Foden. This is a Peterbilt **349** for such uses as transit mixing, dumping, oil field service and snow ploughing. The cab is made of aluminium and engines of 240 to 350 bhp are offered.

Peterbilt **362** is for 40 tons highway use. The standard specification includes 300 bhp Cummins diesel, nine-speed Fuller gearbox and Rockwell axles. It has an all-steel chassis and aluminium cab, shown here in sleeper form with wind deflector.

Peterbilt **359** conventional can have engines of 230 to 600 bhp and Allison, Fuller or Spicer gearboxes. The cab is of aluminium and is shown here in day form. Peterbilt or Hendrickson tandems are offered.

Foden in Britain builds 4 × 2, 6 × 4, 6 × 6, 8 × 4 and 8 × 6 trucks. For 38-tonne operation it advocates light weight 6 × 4 tractive units like this **S106T** with a wide choice of mechanical specification and rubber rear suspension. Foden uses engines by Rolls-Royce, Cummins, Caterpillar and Gardner.

Foden makes various 6 × 4, 6 × 6, 8 × 4 and 8 × 6 trucks for NATO use. Most have Rolls-Royce diesels, like this 220 bhp 6 × 4 12,000 litre tanker.

A Foden assembly company in South Africa makes about two hundred specialist trucks per year using locally available cabs and engines (including Cummins and Atlantis).

Peugeot-Citroen-Talbot

Peugeot acquired Citroen in 1974 (and temporarily along with it, Berliet—see Renault). Both Peugeot and Citroen make light van ranges. In 1978 they acquired Chrysler's European interests and named many of the subsequent products Talbot, though the Dodge interests later came under Renault control. Some of the group's larger vans are related to the Fiat Sevel range produced in Italy.

Citroen **C25** and **C35** vans. The C25 has transverse engine whilst the larger has longitudinal 2 litre petrol or 2·5 litre diesel engine. Load capacity is from 1 to 1·9 tonnes.

Renault

France's only major producer of heavy vehicles is Renault, which in the 1950s created SAVIEM from its own commercial vehicle department plus Latil, Somua and others. In 1974 it added Berliet and has marketed all its trucks as Renaults in recent years. In 1978 it bought a major stake in Mack, followed by American Motors, the makers of Jeeps. In 1981 it took control of Peugeot-Citroen's British and Spanish Dodge factories. It has several other overseas plants, including a joint arrangement with Leyland in Morocco, and holds a home market sales share of about one third.

G230 and **G290** are made in France and also assembled in Britain. The G range includes 5·5, 8·8 and 9·8 litre engine options and 6- to 16-ratio gearboxes. The example shown has a 290 bhp turbo diesel and is for 38 tonne GCW. A twin steer version is also made in Britain.

R390 Turboleader is developed from a former Berliet model and has a V-8 turbo intercooled 390 bhp 14·9 litre diesel. It has an eighteen-speed gearbox plus two crawler ratios. Two- and three-axle versions are made for GVW up to 26 tonnes and GTW up to 180 tonnes.

Some rugged Berliet export models continue in the range. This **GBH260** is for GTW of up to 80 tonnes and has a 220 bhp normally aspirated six-cylinder diesel. This one has 6 × 4 but 6 × 6 is available.

Latest in the French normal control **C** range is the 6 × 4 tipper with 260 bhp turbo diesel. It is for 26 tonnes GVW and 60 tonnes GCW and can have Renault or ZF eight-speed gearboxes, each with an additional crawler ratio. 4 × 2 and 4 × 4 versions are also made.

From the Spanish range comes this **D3464** 6 × 4 tipper. This style of cab was first used on Barreiros trucks which became Dodges with the Chrysler takeover. The factory subsequently came under Peugeot and then Renault control. This one is for 26 tonnes GVW and has an 11·95 litre diesel.

Renault supplies Mack in America with conventional and cab over types in the weight range below Mack's own trucks. This is a **Mid-Liner MS 300T** with charge-cooled 215 bhp Renault diesel.

From Mack's own range, this is an **RD686S.** The RD models can have diesels from 237 to 500 bhp and GVW to 46·7 tonnes. The cab is of galvanized steel.

This low-cab **MR** model has a 235 bhp Mack diesel and five-speed Mack gearbox. It is shown in typical guise with a front operating refuse bin loader. The chassis is also commonly used in the construction industry.

Mack **Ultra-Liner** is from the MH series and has a Mack 300 bhp diesel and five-speed gearbox. Most of the other components are also by Mack, though proprietary engines and other items are available in some specifications.

Mack Super Liner II conventional with sleeping compartment and 'West Coast' fittings. A wide choice of engine and transmission options is listed. Note the Mack Bulldog mascot on mirrors and radiator.

In 1973 Commer and Karrier had come under the control of Chrysler, who already owned British Dodge. In 1976 the Commer name was replaced by Dodge and this is still used despite the Peugeot-Citroen takeover and subsequent Renault control. This is a British **Dodge Commando 2** from a range that can have Perkins six-cylinder or V-8 diesels of 98 to 170 bhp, and is available in 4 × 2, 6 × 2 and 6 × 4 versions. Four-, five- or six-speed synchro gearboxes are offered.

Scania

Scania-Vabis merged with the Saab aeronautics and car firm in 1969 and henceforth their trucks and buses were known as Scanias. In the mid-1980s Scania was making 22,000 vehicles per year at its main factories in Sweden, and in Holland, Brazil, Argentina and Australia. Its five largest markets in order of importance are Brazil, Britain, Iran, Sweden and France. Scania makes some of the most powerful standard trucks in Europe. It severed financial ties with Sisu in 1986 but still uses some joint components.

Scania **P82M** 4 × 2 RS has a GVW of 16·26 tonnes and Scania 210 bhp diesel with five-speed gearbox and splitter. GTW with drawbar trailer is up to 34·5 tonnes.

Scania **P92M** 6 × 2 RC28 is for 38 tonnes GTW and has
Scania 8·5 litre turbo intercooled 275 bhp diesel, five-
speed synchro gearbox with splitter. The P in the des-
ignation means medium cab, other versions being G for
low and R for high.

A Scania **R142MA** 4 × 2 RC running at 38 tonnes GCW,
though the model is suitable for up to 52 tonnes GCW
where permissible. It has a Scania V-8 14·2 litre turbo
intercooled 420 bhp diesel with five-speed synchro
gearbox plus splitter.

A Scania **T112H** 6 × 4 harvesting sugar cane in Réunion. It has an 11 litre 333 bhp diesel and five-speed synchro gearbox plus splitter. Similar trucks with the 14·2 litre engine are suitable for 120 tonnes GTW.

Working in New Zealand carrying bales of wool is a Scania **R142H** 8 × 4 with drawbar trailer. It has a 14·2 litre 420 bhp turbo intercooled diesel. The rigid eight most commonly seen in Europe has the 8·5 litre engine.

Toyota

The Japanese Toyota company and GMC of America vie for the position of largest producer of vehicles in the world. Toyota makes light and medium commercials under its own name. It also controls the light vehicle maker Daihatsu and the Hino heavy truck firm. Toyota has assembly plants in 20 countries and Hino has them in 36. Hino has 8,000 employees engaged solely on heavy commercial vehicles and is believed to be second only to Mercedes-Benz in heavy truck output, selling about 65,000 per year, whilst Toyota has 45,000 employees in Japan, including its car making factories.

Toyota **Dyna** range includes 2 and 2·4 litre petrol models and 3 and 4 litre diesel models. This is a 4·3 tonne GVW crewcab version with 2 or 3 litre engine and five-speed gearbox. All have tilt-cabs.

Toyota 11·5 tonne GVW model has 6·5 litre six-cylinder
148 bhp diesel and five-speed gearbox, with single- or
two-speed rear axle.

Hino NZ normal control 4 × 2 or 4 × 4 model is for up
to 16 tonne GVW. It has a 9·4 litre six-cylinder 215 bhp
diesel with six-speed synchro gearbox plus two speed
transfer box on the 4 × 4 shown.

Hino FD Econo Diesel models have 150 or 165 bhp engines and five-speed synchro gearboxes. GVW is 9·9 tonnes. The tilt-cab, like so many rival vehicles in this weight range, has car-like driving controls.

Hino SH series can have 260 or 320 bhp diesels and are for GCW of up to 40 tonnes. Six- or nine-speed synchro gearboxes are used. There are also SS three-axle versions.

80

Volvo

Volvo is the largest Swedish producer of trucks and is second only to Mercedes-Benz in Europe as a whole. It has additional factories in Britain, Peru, Switzerland, Belgium, Morocco, Brazil, Australia and elsewhere, and has owned White and Autocar in America since 1981. It sold 40,800 trucks in 1984, of which 9,400 were Whites and Autocars. White also assembles some Volvo models in America, and itself uses some Volvo engines in addition to the usual proprietary makes. In the crane-carrier and construction industry section will be found Volvo-BM and Kockum dumptrucks, the latter firm having belonged to Volvo since 1983.

Volvo **F408,** built in Ghent, Belgium, has 125 bhp six-cylinder turbo diesel and five-speed synchromesh gearbox. GVW is 7·5 tonnes. The model, which has a tilt cab, is only built with left-hand drive at present.

New in 1985 were the FL6, FL7 and FL10. The F indicates forward control whilst the L signifies low-built. They range in power from 152 to 299 bhp and have galvanized steel tilt cabs. The smallest 11-ton version has disc brakes on both axles. Shown is an **FL10** with 299 bhp six-cylinder diesel and eight- or sixteen-speed gearbox for up to 44 tonnes GCW.

Built in Britain for the Swiss market is the ultra-narrow (2·3 m) **CH320** 8 × 4. Two-, three- and four-axle versions are available with 330 bhp six-cylinder diesels and sixteen-speed gearboxes. Note the Trilex type wheels with demountable rims that are popular in North America and Switzerland.

The Volvo F10 and F12 series covers two-, three- and four-axle trucks covering GVW of 16·5 to 33·5 tonnes or GTW of up to 100 tonnes. This **F10** has an intercooled turbo 9·6 litre 299 bhp diesel and eight-speed synchro gearbox. It is shown in day cab form with wind foil. Sleeper and raised roof Globetrotter cabs are also available.

The N range covers normal control (conventional) models like this **N12** turbo intercooled 4 × 2 artic unit. It has a 12-litre diesel developing 385 bhp and nine or fourteen gear ratios. GVW is 19·5 tonnes and GTW of over 100 tonnes is feasible.

White continue to make trucks in Utah and Virginia using typical American proprietary components. Like Volvos made in America they have bolted chassis construction. This **High Cabover** has Cummins 300 bhp diesel, nine-speed Fuller gearbox and Rockwell axles.

White Conventional with integral sleeper cab normally has Cummins 300 or 400 bhp diesels and Fuller thirteen-speed gearbox. Air suspension on the rear Rockwell tandem is optional. The high specification cab interior includes simulated leather and woodgrain.

White Expeditor comes in 4 × 2 and 6 × 4 versions and is primarily for local delivery work. Standard engine is 240 bhp Cummins with Allison automatic transmission and Rockwell axles. The forward-set cab eases access on multiple stop-start work.

Autocar makes the specialist on and off highway trucks for Volvo White in America. This is its conventional **DS** 6 × 4 highway mixer chassis. It is powered by a 400 bhp Cummins diesel with Fuller thirteen-speed gearbox and Rockwell axles.

SPECIALIST MANUFACTURERS

On-highway Haulage

The major groups and their associates looked at in the previous section produce the majority of the world's trucks. However, there are several smaller individual firms or groups that concentrate on a more limited range of trucks or on particular markets. In the following pages we show some of those which make successful on-highway types, often using familiar proprietary components that are also used by some of their bigger and less specialist rivals. Several of the firms of course also make other types of truck and some will be found in later sections.

AVM-Dahmer CD750 made in Harare, Zimbabwe is for 30 tonnes GCW and has a DAF 156 bhp diesel and ZF six-speed constant mesh gearbox. Its makers are owned by the broad-based British Lonhro company. Other models include six-wheelers for up to 55 tonnes GCW.

Diamond Reo is a combination of two famous American names that belonged to White for a time. They became jointly independent once more in the mid 1970s and are made by Osterlund Inc, Harrisburg, PA. All their models are called Giants and can have a wide choice of proprietary components.

Diamond Reo **Giant C11664D** has choice of Cummins 240 to 400 bhp diesels and Fuller transmissions. It has a galvanized steel cab and Rockwell axles rated for 6 tons front and 20 tons tandem.

The increasingly popular droop-nose styling seen on many American conventionals is employed on the Diamond Reo **Giant C11664DD**. It has a Deutz 315 bhp diesel and Fuller gearbox.

One of Britain's most popular heavy trucks is the ERF, made in Sandbach, Cheshire (and also in South Africa) by a firm that has produced over 50,000 trucks since its foundation in 1933. This is an example of its 1986 **E Series**. E10/E14 indicate Cummins 10/14 litre diesels.

Part of a fleet of ERF 6 × 4 tractive units destined for Saudi Arabia. They normally have Cummins 350 bhp engines though a South African version has the locally produced Atlantis 280 bhp diesel.

ERFs use steel framed tilt cab with SMC panels. This is a 31 tonne GVW 8 × 4 tipper powered by a Gardner 270 bhp diesel. Cummins and Rolls-Royce engines are also available.

Marmon 57L lightweight tractor weighs under 6 tons thanks to aluminium cab and wheels with fibreglass hood and fenders. It has a Caterpillar diesel, Fuller gearbox and very unusual feature of Rockwell disc brakes.

KMC trucks produced in Cyprus and feature cabs and other components from many trucks. This one might at first appear to be a MAN, and indeed a MAN 215 bhp diesel is offered though an alternative is a 228 bhp Detroit with ZF manual or Allison automatic transmission. Some other models are Dodge or Dennis based.

Leader trucks are made in Towoomba, Queensland, Australia and include cab over and conventional models. This example has Sundowner fibreglass sleeper cab and choice of Caterpillar or Detroit diesels and Fuller gearbox. Several three- and four-axle models are produced.

Best known as a shipbuilder, Hollming of Finland has a factory at Kankaanpaa making 6 × 2 road tankers with integral construction. This reduces height and weight, especially as horizontal underfloor MAN 11·4 litre or Volvo 9·6 litre diesels are used with Volvo 8-speed splitter gearboxes. With a trailer 37,500 litres of liquid can be carried.

A well-known Mexican firm, Trailers de Monterrey, added tractive units made from proprietary components in 1959. Its current **Ramirez R-22** has Cummins 350 or 450 bhp or Detroit 430 bhp diesels, Spicer 14-ratio gearbox and Hendrickson tandem. GVW is 26 tonnes.

Best known for its fire appliances and municipal vehicles, Hestair Dennis of Guildford, England, also makes this Dennis **Delta 16** with Perkins 158 bhp or Gardner 180 bhp diesels and six-speed synchro gearbox. It is for 16·26 tonne GVW and has a steel, fibreglass and aluminium tilt cab.

The **Sonacome C230** is made in Rouiba, Algeria by a factory that started in 1957 as a branch of Berliet (see Renault). This 6 × 4 tipper has a 230 bhp diesel. The former Berliet operation in Morocco is now run jointly by Renault and Leyland.

Tata is a major Indian industrial group whose interests include steel, power stations, farm tractors, road making machinery and trucks. The latter were originally based on Mercedes-Benz designs. This is a **PPTW-1312** chassis/scuttle awaiting bodywork. A normal control type can be seen in the off-highway section.

Premier trucks made in India include this 12·2 tonne GVW Perkins 120 bhp engined Roadmaster **PFR-122SF.** Their local rivals include Ashok (see Leyland), Shakti (see MAN), plus Tata and Hindustan (in this section).

Western Star is a Canadian firm formed in 1981 from part of the White empire. This conventional 6 × 4 with sleeping compartment can have Caterpillar, Cummins or Detroit diesels of 210 to 525 bhp and Fuller or Spicer gearboxes.

Western Star aluminium cab-over has same engine and transmission options as conventional. Western Star also makes various logging and other on/off highway types.

Hindustan J6 made in India is based on a Bedford design and is for 11·2 tonnes GVW. It has a 5·4 litre 112 bhp diesel engine (petrol optional) and four- or five-speed gearbox. Similar Bedford-based vehicles are made in Turkey by Genoto, some with Mercedes-Benz-licence diesels.

Loheac **TLH 2175** is for 19 tonnes GVW/38 tonnes GCW and can have DAF, Scania or Renault diesels with Fuller gearboxes. It is made by a French haulage firm primarily for its own requirements and has a fibreglass tilt cab.

Terberg of Benschop, Holland makes various specialist vehicles. Its highway range includes municipal vehicles, tippers and front wheel drive skip collectors. This 6 × 4 low-loader has a Volvo cab and 330 bhp engine, Fuller 13-speed gearbox and Soma rear axles.

The French Sovam company makes various specialized vehicles, notably for loading aircraft. It also produces Etalmobil local delivery vehicles. This example opens out into a travelling shop and uses Renault mechanical components.

The major maker of trucks in Finland is Sisu of Karjaa. This is its **SK21OCKH** 6 × 2 with Cummins L10 diesel and Fuller 13-speed gearbox.

The Sisu **SR** series has a Cummins 14-litre diesel and Fuller 13-speed gearbox. For routine maintenance the bonnet provides access but for major work the cab also tilts forward. The unusual 8 × 2· layout provides two steering axles.

Sisu **SM 260 CKH** 6 × 2 Finlandia has Cummins 14-litre diesel in various degrees of turbocharging up to 350 bhp, and Fuller 13-speed gearbox. GVW is 27 tonnes and GCW is 70 tonnes.

Well-known British electric vehicle makers include Electricar of Atherstone, Smith's of Gateshead and W&E of Shrewsbury. This is the last named's 6/80, able to carry four tonnes at over 20 mph.

FTF trucks from Wijchen, Holland use Detroit diesels, Motor Panels of Coventry tilt cabs and Fuller or Allison gearboxes. This **FD/FS 7.20 TLS** 6 × 2 is for 18·3 tonnes GVW, plus trailer.

Titan of Appenweier, West Germany, makes mostly off-highway and heavy haulage units but it can undertake many types of specialist vehicles like this distribution truck based on Mercedes-Benz components. The frame has been built over the container space to allow interchangeable bodies to be raised and locked to it.

This four tonne capacity **Puma** built in Brazil has a fibreglass tilt cab and choice of Perkins or MWM 83 bhp diesels, with Clark gearboxes and Brazilian Rockwell drive-axle.

Most of Pacific's output in Canada is off-highway or ultra-heavy types. However, it does offer conventional highway models like this 'Canadian' **P-500-F.** Its cab is by International with Pacific's own fibreglass bonnet and choice of engines from Cummins, Detroit or Caterpillar.

Like Pacific, most of Hendrickson's output in Lyons, Illinois is of special types, but it does offer highway conventionals like this **H-3-38-C13** with Rockwell axles, steel cab, Fuller 13-speed gearbox and Cummins 300 bhp diesel. 280 to 445 bhp engines by Caterpillar, Cummins and Detroit can be employed.

Construction Industry Trucks

Standard heavy duty trucks cope with many site haulage jobs and vehicles for tipping, girder and plant transport, skip lifting, concrete mixing, etc., are shown in other sections. Here we concentrate on a small random selection of the trucks evolved specially for their role in the construction or mineral extraction industries. Many are so large that they are totally impracticable for road use, whilst others are cleverly adapted to road regulations for moving massive permanently mounted cranes from site to site. Later in this section are some of the dozens of different dumptrucks available; for a more complete listing see *Giant Dumptrucks* by Nick Baldwin (Haynes Publishing).

In Italy, Astra and a firm called CVS, formed by a break-away group of employees, make dumptrucks and crane carriers. This is a **CVS** 6 × 6 chassis with Fiat diesel; it is designed to be fitted with a crane.

Some truck firms like Faun and Hendrickson make just the chassis to which crane superstructures are fitted. Others, like Coles and Lokomo, make the complete units. This **Lokomo** has a 300 bhp Volvo driving unit and another Volvo engine on the crane.

SFB of Langenfeld, West Germany, makes chassis for cranes and concrete pumps with 285 to 400 bhp diesels. Just the front portion of this 8 × 4 is shown with one of its integral outriggers in place.

Hendrickson of Lyons, Illinois, makes many types of special chassis for such duties as concrete pumping, seismic exploration, crane carrying and, as in this instance, drilling rig transport. It has a 216 bhp diesel, 13-speed gearbox and 8 × 4.

Mitsubishi is relatively unusual in being a high volume truck manufacturer that also offers specialist chassis. It makes crane carriers for machines with lifting capacities of 15 to 150 tons with 215 to 310 bhp diesels.

Faun in West Germany makes one of the widest ranges of crane carrier, with engines of 192 to 560 bhp and three to eight axles. On this example all six axles can be steered.

Oshkosh S series forward placement concrete mixers allow the driver to see exactly what he is doing. They have rear mounted Cummins or Detroit 240 to 330 bhp diesels and are basically 6 × 6 machines, sometimes with one or two additional tag axles.

The Chuting Star made by Forward Inc. of Huron, South Dakota, is a 6 × 6 rear engined, front placement mixer with Detroit or Cummins diesels of 238 to 335 bhp and Allison automatic transmission.

Various firms make special open frame skip lifters. Amongst them are Terberg, and Spliess of Magdeburg, East Germany. This is the latter's 5 tonne capacity **Tramp** 4 × 4 with Robur 70 bhp diesel and five-speed gearbox.

There are numerous manufacturers of pivot-steer dumptrucks, of which perhaps the best known are DJB and Volvo-BM. Here we have a Dutch rival in the shape of a **Werklust WD3**. It is for 32 tonne loads and has 6 × 6, Detroit 260 bhp diesel and Allison torque converter transmission.

Smallest in the Italian Perlini dumptruck range is the **DP 255** for 25 tonne loads. Fiat or Detroit 300 bhp diesels are offered with Allison automatic transmission.

Unit Rig makes diesel-electric dumptrucks and Dart makes mechanical-drive trucks in the Kendavis Industries group of Fort Worth. This is Unit Rig's largest 172·4 tonne capacity truck with choice of 16-cylinder Detroit or Cummins 1800 bhp diesels. It has rubber suspension and General Electric traction motor. Height untipped is 6·15 metres.

6 × 4 trucks are able to have more traction and a lower centre of gravity than giant 4 × 2s. This **Dart 2085** is for 77 tonne loads. Cummins or Detroit 800 bhp diesels are offered with Allison transmissions. Rimpull make similar trucks to 1050 bhp.

Dart **3120** is a 109 tonne capacity rear dumptruck with Allison transmission and choice of Cummins or Detroit engines from 1050 to 1350 bhp. Suspension is by rubber blocks with radius rods.

Haulamatic Clarke Chapman Ltd., of Heanor, England, makes three-axle rigid and two- and three-axle pivot-steer dumptrucks. They are available with Detroit diesels and Allison transmissions. This 4 × 4 can carry 18·2 tonnes.

Kaelble of Backnang, West Germany, makes rigid and articulated dumptrucks of up to 45 tonnes capacity. This is its 580 bhp, 4 × 4, **KK50.**

Rimpull of Olathe, Kansas, makes trucks with triple or quadruple reduction axles. Its coal haulers go up to this 200 tons capacity, Cummins 1200 bhp engined electric transmission bottom dumper.

Caterpillar of Peoria, Illinois, makes many types of construction machinery, including dumptrucks. This is their **773B** for 45·4 tonne loads. It uses a Caterpillar V-12 650 bhp diesel and Caterpillar seven forward speed automatic transmission. Caterpillar uses oil immersed disc brakes with independent oleo-pneumatic suspension and its largest two-axle rigid has a GVW of 230·5 tonnes and a 1380 bhp diesel.

Euclid has belonged in recent years to GMC, White and Daimler-Benz. Since 1984 Clark Michigan has run it and this is its **R-35** for 32 tonne loads. It has Detroit or Cummins 450 bhp diesels, Allison transmission, and disc brakes.

Euclid R-170 has diesel-electric drive with Cummins, Detroit or MTU 1600 bhp diesels. Payload is 154 tonnes. As with many dumptrucks the exhaust gases warm the body walls for easier load discharge.

Wabco has made Haulpak dumptrucks since 1957. This **170D** has a 1600 bhp Cummins or Detroit diesel driving twin electric wheel motors. It has oleo-nitrogen suspension and is for 154 tonne loads.

Wabco 3200B diesel-electric dumptruck has a General Motors EMD 127 litre 2475 bhp two-stroke, twelve-cylinder diesel and can carry 227 tonnes within a GVW of 393 tonnes. It has hydro-pneumatic suspension and compressed air starting.

A recent arrival on the American giant dumptruck scene is the Wiseda 'King of the Lode'. It can carry 220 tons and has a 2450 bhp diesel.

The Japanese Komatsu firm makes various dumptrucks including this 160 tonne capacity machine with automatic transmission and Cummins V-16 50·3 litre 1600 bhp diesel. It has hydro-pneumatic suspension and oil-cooled disc brakes.

Various heavy dumptrucks are produced in Comecon countries. DAC in Romania offers 50 and 100 tonne capacity two axle trucks and this is a 380 bhp Russian **Belaz 540A** for 30 tonne loads.

China makes various sizes of dumptruck using American, British and Russian design features. This is a **Jiefang CA390** with 720 bhp V-12 diesel for 60 tonne loads. Other types can carry up to 100 tonnes. Aveling Barford sold a £50 million five-year dumptruck development programme to China in the mid 1980s.

Made in Peterlee, England, using many Caterpillar mechanical components is the pivot-steer DJB **D550.** It has a 460 bhp diesel and can carry 50 tonnes. The front and centre axles are driven.

DJB claims to be the world's largest makers of heavy duty pivot-steer haulers. This is their **D35HP.** It has a Caterpillar 385 bhp diesel, planetary powershift transmission and 4 × 4. Payload is 31·8 tonnes.

Heathfield of Newton Abbot, England make 18 and 30 tonne capacity dumptrucks. This is the smaller **H20C** with Cummins 235 bhp diesel and Fuller five-speed gearbox. It has rubber suspension, independent at the front.

Volvo-BM **5350** has 213 bhp, 6·73 litre diesel and five-speed torque converter transmission. The front and centre axles are driven and have disc brakes. Payload is 20 tonnes and the 5350 has pivot-steering.

Volvo-BM has owned the makers of Kockum rigid dumptrucks since 1983. This is their **540** model which has recently been rebadged Volvo-BM. It has a 456 bhp Cummins diesel with Allison transmission and is for 36·3 tonne loads.

Terex is the name used by GM for its dumptrucks following the sale of its Euclid division. For a time in the early 1980s Terex was run by the German IBH group. GM dumptrucks built in Canada are called Titans. This is an **R-17 Terex** made in Motherwell, Scotland for 15·42 tonne loads. It has Detroit 238 bhp or Cummins 220 bhp diesels and five-speed Fuller gearbox.

This is the largest Terex two-axle rigid, the **33.14** for 109 tonne loads. It has a Detroit 1,200 bhp V-12 diesel and Allison transmission. Terex now also makes a 6 × 6 pivot-steer truck which can be seen in the off-highway section. The largest Terex built to date has a 3300 bhp diesel and is for 350 ton loads.

General Motors of Canada makes this **Terex 33-15C** which has recently been renamed Titan. It is a diesel-electric truck with Detroit or Cummins 1600 bhp diesels driving twin GM 750 bhp electric motors. It is for 258 tonnes GVW and 154 tonnes payload.

The well-known British Aveling Barford construction machinery firm joined the Leyland group in 1967 and was sold to an American businessman in 1983. This is its **RD 017** with Leyland 200 bhp diesel with five forward and three reverse gears and reversible controls. GVW is 27 tonnes.

Aveling Barford **RXD 025** is for 25 tonne loads and has 6 × 4, Caterpillar 210 bhp diesel and Allison automatic gearbox. It has disc brakes and suspension by air at the front and rubber at the rear.

Aveling Barford **RD 150** has Cummins or Detroit 600 bhp diesels with Allison transmission and nitrogen-oil suspension. Payload is 45·4 tonnes.

Special low-profile 8 × 8 transporters for pipeline laying are made by Terberg, Semex, Canadian Foremost, etc. This **Terberg** is 18·6 metres long, has steering on all wheels, a Volvo 350 bhp diesel, and is for 80 tonnes GVW.

DJB dumptruck haulage units are also used on pipeline work. This is a 35 tonne capacity model with Caterpillar 260 bhp diesel. It has 4 × 4 and high-flotation tyres.

121

MOL of Hooglede, Belgium, makes all manner of specialist vehicles. This is a crane-carrier chassis with Deutz air-cooled diesel. 6 × 4, 6 × 6, 8 × 4, 8 × 6, 10 × 6 and 12 × 6 versions for cranes weighing 15 to 130 tons are offered.

This MOL 6 × 6 is equipped with a drilling rig and has a Deutz 12·8 litre air-cooled 250 bhp diesel and ZF gearbox with Timken axles. Capacity of the chassis is 18 tonnes.

Semex of Dorsten, West Germany, makes 8 × 8 chassis with central backbone chassis using Tatra components. They are used for cranes, drilling rigs, tree planters and pipe transport. This **36270** model has Tatra 400 bhp air-cooled diesel and ZF gearbox.

Canadian Foremost **Husky 8** has Detroit or Cummins 350 bhp diesels and Allison automatic transmission. Pneumatic tyres run within the four rubber belt tracks. Payload is 36·3 tonnes and GVW 76·7 tonnes.

Canadian Foremost **Magnum 4** pipe transporter has 104·4 tonne GVW and 8 × 8. Detroit or Cummins 465 bhp diesels drive Clark eight forward four reverse ratio power shift gearbox. To steer the machine the frame is pivoted at the centre.

Canadian Foremost makes various chassis for cranes and drilling rigs ranging from 22·7 to 45·4 tonnes GVW. They can have Cummins, Caterpillar or Detroit 175 to 600 bhp diesels and manual or automatic transmission.

The **Oshkosh F-2538** is basically a 6 × 6 chassis. It is shown here in use as a concrete block transporter with additional pusher and tag axles to reduce highway weight loadings. Cummins and Caterpillar 210 to 270 bhp engines can be specified with Fuller 9- or 10-speed gearboxes.

The Pacific **P-12-W** 6 × 4 chassis with 475 bhp Detroit diesel and Allison six-speed power shift transmission is available for various heavy-duty tasks, in this case carrying 40 tons of coal from a strip mine. It has a Clark tandem and Rockwell front axle.

Faun makes a range of 22 to 77 tonne capacity two-axle dumptrucks powered by Deutz, Cummins or Detroit diesels of 250 to 900 bhp. Most have Allison transmissions, though a ZF manual gearbox is available on the smallest. Shown is a 50 tonne capacity 635 bhp Cummins engined **K55.6.**

Astra makes crane carriers, dumptrucks, transit mixers and other specialist chassis in Piacenza, Italy. This is its **BM35** with Detroit 456 bhp diesel and Allison transmission. It has a 24 m³ rock body for 35 tonne loads.

Astra **BM20** can have Fiat or Mercedes-Benz 260 bhp diesels and six- or nine-speed gearboxes. This is a 6 × 4 for 21·45 tonnes and a 6 × 6 version is also offered.

Moxy D16B Super made in Elnesvågen, Norway, is a pivot steer, 6 × 6 machine for loads of up to 22 tonnes. It has a Scania 210 bhp turbo diesel and Clark power shift transmission.

Cline of Kansas City, USA, makes road-rail trucks, crane carriers and various dumptrucks. This is its **25R** with Cummins or Detroit 250 bhp diesels and Allison or Fuller gearboxes. Payload is 25 tons.

CCC of Tulsa, USA specializes in crane carriers, refuse chassis and forward or rear discharge concrete mixer chassis. This is its **Century II** 6 × 4 with Cummins, Detroit or Caterpillar diesels and Fuller or Spicer gearboxes.

Trailer Spotters

These are produced for various forms of localized towing and often have half-cabs for maximum visibility. Many spend all their lives moving trailers in yards and docks, where they have to be compatible with all manner and size of equipment. To achieve this ro-ro (roll on roll off ferry types) have variable turntable height. Amongst the many worldwide producers are American-Coleman, Ibex, Terberg, MAFI, Douglas, Reliance-Mercury, Hendrickson, Sisu, MOL, Kalmar and Ottawa.

American-Coleman Yard Horse made in Littleton, Colorado, is for 48 tons GTW and can have Detroit, Cummins or Caterpillar diesels of 140 to 210 bhp. Allison five-speed automatic gearboxes are used.

Douglas of Cheltenham, England makes a wide assortment of Tugmaster ro-ro tractors and aircraft and industrial tugs. This is an **N58** Yard Shunter with choice of
124 bhp Perkins or 165 bhp Detroit diesels with Allison
automatic transmission. A 6 × 4 version also with ele-
vating fifth wheel is offered.

The West German **MAFI** half-cab tractor uses components, including six-cylinder diesel, made by Volvo.

Reliance-Mercury Haulmajor made in Halifax, England has Leyland 160/180 bhp, Volvo 180 bhp or Mercedes-Benz 216 bhp diesels. Some have all-wheel drive for maximum traction.

MOL, whose off-road vehicles are shown elsewhere, makes 4 × 4 and 4 × 2 terminal tractors using DAF axles and diesels and Allison gearboxes.

The Ottawa Truck Corp of Ottawa, Kansas, makes two- and three-axle tractors with Ford, Caterpillar, Detroit or Cummins engines of 165 to 210 bhp. Some have additional flanged wheels for railroad operation.

Hendrickson of Chicago is another firm to offer trailer spotters. Caterpillar, Cummins and Detroit diesels of approximately 210 bhp are offered with Allison transmissions. The trailer lift has a 35 tons rating. It makes numerous other special-purpose trucks.

Sisu makes Volvo engined trailer spotters in Finland.
This one has reversible driver's controls and 4 × 4. It is
powered by a six-cylinder 215 bhp turbo diesel and is
shown with its fifth wheel raised.

Ibex of Salt Lake City, USA makes specialist vehicles
including scissor-lifts for supplying aircraft. This is its
F-2 Terminal Tractor with choice of Ford, Detroit,
Caterpillar or Cummins 145 to 215 bhp engines and
Allison transmission.

Off-highway Trucks

Whilst examining the products of the major multi-national firms we have seen that several are available with all-wheel drive. This increases their ability to work off metalled highways. Under the crane-carrier and construction truck section are shown several vehicles for specific off-highway tasks. Now we look at an assortment of general purpose all-wheel drive trucks not so far represented, starting with some military types.

Bombardier of Valcourt, Canada made tracked and wheeled off-highway types including the former VW Iltis. This is their 4·5 tonne (2·3 tonne cross country) capacity 6 × 6 with GM Bedford 165 bhp diesel and Allison transmission.

The **Esarco** 8 × 8 made by Laird (Anglesey) Ltd, uses many Land-Rover components including V-8 petrol engine, transmission and axles.

Oshkosh MK48 is an 8 × 8 pivot-steer truck with GVW of 39·2 tonnes. it has a Detroit 445 bhp V-8 diesel and Allison automatic torque converter transmission. It can climb a sixty per cent gradient with full load.

Though visually similar to the previous truck and using a similar engine and transmission, this Oshkosh 8 × 8 steers on each front axle and not at its frame centre. GVW goes up to 43 tonnes depending on model. Several thousand have been ordered by the US Army.

Representing the Comecon block (other examples of whose off-highway types are shown in the first section) we have a **FAP 2026 BS/AV** 6 × 6. It can carry six tonnes cross-country or ten tonnes on the road and has a six-speed synchro gearbox. It has a Mercedes-Benz licence 256 bhp V-8 diesel and cab.

Federal Motors of Ocala, USA makes fire appliance, utility and various 4 × 4 and 6 × 6 cross-country chassis. This is an example of its 4 × 4 armoured model.

Terex of Motherwell, Scotland, make this **2366 LC** 20 tonne capacity pivot-steer 6 × 6. It has a Deutz 227 bhp air-cooled diesel and ZF torque converter six-speed gearbox.

Many Russian vehicles are made with an all-wheel drive option but this 8 × 8 is a specific military type. It is a **MAZ 543** for 15 tonne loads with 525 bhp V-12 diesel and torque converter transmission.

Another Comecon type, this time a 4 × 4 version of a Star civilian truck made in Poland. It has a 6·84 litre six-cylinder diesel, five-speed synchro gearbox and is for 5 tonne loads plus a trailer of 8·5 tonnes gross weight.

ALM Acmat military trucks are made in France and feature Perkins diesel engines. Payload of this **VLRA** is 4·3 tonnes. Its 135 bhp diesel drives through a five-speed gearbox and two-speed transfer box.

Leaving specifically military trucks, we have an example of a type of 4 × 4 transporter made by numerous firms in and around the Alps. This is a **Ferrari 933** made in Italy. It has a payload of two tonnes and a two-cylinder 50 bhp diesel with eleven forward and six reverse ratio gearbox.

For optimum flotation of heavy loads over soft ground tracked carriers come into their own. This is a **Bombardier** made in Canada, where the type is widely used on muskeg.

Long distance rallies in arduous terrain frequently attract 4 × 4 trucks. This is a 1985 contender in the Paris–Dakar event. It is a **Liaz** 4·2 tonne capacity **11.124D** with 11·94 litre 340 bhp diesel.

There are numerous American specialist producers of off-highway trucks. This one looks similar to the WD pattern Eager Beaver or the current NATO 2·5 tonners as exemplified by Bombardier. However, it is in fact a **Paramount P2000** 6 × 6 for civilian roles with fibre-glass one-piece bonnet moulding.

Many firms offer 4 × 4 versions of standard 4 × 2 high-way models. Even if they do not, there are various specialists able to convert them. This is an example of a 4 × 4 **Indian Tata.**

TMU vehicles are made in Bilbao, Spain, and include 6 × 6 and 8 × 8 types. This is a special **6675 Forestal** model with winch for timber extraction. It has a Pegaso 200 bhp diesel and five-speed two-range gearbox. GVW is 26 tonnes.

Diamond Reo Giant makes 6 × 6 and 4 × 4 models in its conventional range. This one has a Cummins 240 bhp diesel, Fuller gearbox, Dana Spicer transfer box and Rockwell axles.

Most Jeeps and Land-Rovers are below the payload limit of this book but larger versions of both are made around the world. This is Mahindra's variation on the FC Jeep theme with 72 bhp petrol engine or alternative Perkins diesel. GVW is 3·3 tonnes.

Canadian Foremost **Delta Three** has Terra Tyres and 6 × 6. It uses Detroit 197 bhp or Cummins 189 bhp diesels and Clark powershift torque converter transmission. It has pivot-steer and 26·5 tonnes GVW.

Canadian Foremost's largest wheeled truck is the pivot-steer 8 × 8 **Super Commander C** with Cummins 525 bhp diesel and Clark eight-speed torque converter transmission. Payload is 36·3 tonnes and GVW 74·9 tonnes.

MOL of Hooglede, Belgium, makes this 13·3 tonne capacity pivot-steer 6 × 6 **Buggy.** It has a 250 bhp Deutz air-cooled diesel and six-speed synchro gearbox. It has disc brakes on all axles.

This **MOL HFT644** chassis equipped with desert tyres is for 2·9 tonne loads of oil exploration equipment. It has a Deutz 120 bhp air-cooled diesel, five-speed Fuller gearbox and two-speed Wisconsin transfer box.

Another Deutz powered MOL, this time a 6 × 6 with winch and narrow centre-mounted cab to enable long pipes and girders to be carried alongside.

MOL T6066/05 is for heavy-duty oilfield work and has a GVW of 60 tonnes and GTW of 135 tonnes. It uses a Deutz twelve-cylinder 432 bhp turbo diesel, Clark torque converter transmission and Kessler planetary reduction axles. The cab is made of steel and fibreglass.

British-built **Boughton RB44** can have Ford, Perkins, Bedford or Rover engines of 85 to 155 bhp and is a 4 × 4 five tonne GVW utilizing a Dodge 50 cab. Reynolds Boughton of Winkleigh, Devon, England, also make fire crash tenders and Rolls-Royce 450 bhp engined 6 × 6 trucks.

146

RAM of Rotterdam makes cross-country trucks using some MAN components. This **1400SF** has a MAN 230 bhp 10·7 litre diesel, ZF six-speed gearbox with Timken transfer box and Timken axles. GVW is 21·7 tonnes and GTW 43 tonnes.

RAM 4 × 4 uses a Renault 133 bhp diesel, ZF five-speed synchro gearbox, MAN axles and MAN tilt cab. GVW is 16 tonnes and GTW is 26 tonnes.

Brimont of Rilly la Montagne, France, took over the old Latil 4 × 4 range from Renault in 1974 and makes 4 × 4 trucks. This is its **Brutt** for 3·5 tonnes GVW with Peugeot 95 bhp diesel.

Brimont TL80 has 4 × 4 and four-wheel steering and is for 12·5 tonnes GVW. It has Perkins or Renault 145 bhp diesels and ZF gearbox. It is shown here with front loader.

148

The Brimont 12·5 tonne GVW **ETR** model is also made in America by the Ottawa Truck Corp of Kansas, where it is called Commando. It has a Mack/Renault 171 bhp diesel and six-speed synchro gearbox with two-speed transfer box. Both axles steer and the chassis is in two sections to allow each portion to oscillate by 15 degrees on uneven ground.

Sisu SL 4 × 4 has a Valmet 170 or 184 cylinder six-cylinder turbo diesel (Cummins optional) and ZF six-speed synchro gearbox. GVW is 20 tonnes and the truck has a three-seat steel cab.

Ginaf of Ederveen, Holland, make 4 × 4, 6 × 6, and 8 × 8 and 10 × 8 trucks. This **F490 DKX** 8 × 8 has a DAF turbo 330 bhp diesel and ZF two range eight-speed synchro gearbox plus transfer box. It has Ginaf and DAF rear tandems and is for 47·4 tonnes GVW.

Petros Petropoulos of Athens makes **Polytrak** and **Militrak** 4 × 4 trucks with Perkins 77 bhp diesels, two range four-speed gearboxes and Dana axles. GVW is 4·5 tonnes.

The Dutch Terberg **F3000** 10 × 8 has a Volvo 320 bhp turbo diesel, Fuller eight-speed gearbox with two-speed transfer box and Terberg/Soma axles. The tilt cab is by Volvo. GVW is 46 tonnes, or up to 55 tonnes off-highway.

Terberg **SF1400** 6 × 4 and SF1300 6 × 6 use Mercedes-Benz cab and 240 bhp engine with Volvo or ZF gearbox. Axles are by Rockwell or ZF. GVW is up to 31 tonnes.

Terberg **SF 1350** is a 6 × 6 truck for 34 tonnes GVW. It has a Volvo cab, Volvo 260 bhp diesel and Volvo eight-speed synchro gearbox plus two-speed transfer box, and Terberg hub reduction axles. A 6 × 4 version is also offered, with Rockwell front and Terberg rear axles.

RFW makes 4 × 4, 6 × 6, 8 × 4 and 8 × 8 trucks in Chester Hill, Australia, with choice of Caterpillar, Cummins or Detroit diesels. Tilt-cabs are fibreglass and steel over a steel frame. This example can cross difficult country to reach a railway and then travel on retractable flanged wheels.

This RFW 6 × 6 has a special fire proof cab with internal steel panelling for work in bush fires. It has Allison automatic transmission and Cummins, Detroit or Caterpillar diesels of approximately 230 bhp. GVW is 30·5 tonnes and GCW 68 tonnes.

Kaelble makes many types of off-highway trucks in West Germany including tractive units and amphibians. This 6 × 6 half-cab truck is for carrying household rubbish from dumping point to landfill sites.

Pacific of North Vancouver is part of the British-based Inchcape Group and makes heavy duty trucks, notably for timber and oil extraction. This 6 × 6 hauling unit, however, is used in the Hawaiian sugar cane industry. It has a 475 bhp Detroit diesel and Clark torque converter transmission.

Russian **Ural 375A** has V-8 7 litre 198 bhp petrol engine and five-speed synchromesh gearbox with two-speed transfer box. Payload is 5 tonnes and the truck's six tyres can have their pressure altered on the move.

154

Russian **MAZ 509A** is a 4 × 4 machine for 10 tonne loads or up to 21 tonnes with semi-trailer. It has a 205 bhp V-6 diesel.

West German **Faun HZ40.45/45** 6 × 6 has Deutz 512 bhp V-12 air-cooled diesel and Fuller or Allison gearboxes. GVW is up to 130 tonnes and GTW 250 tonnes. Faun makes numerous other off-highway types.

Titan of Appenweier, West Germany, makes normal control 6 × 6 off-highway units with diesels of up to 615 bhp. This one has 525 bhp and a sixteen ratio gearbox plus torque converter. GVW is 50 tonnes.

Titan makes 8 × 6 and 8 × 8 forward control models for 48 to 65 tonnes GVW. They have diesels of up to 420 bhp and 8- or 16-speed gearboxes, some with torque converters.

Fire and Municipal Trucks

Several truck makers produce specific chassis for this specialized work. In the case of fire appliances they have more powerful engines than equivalent highway trucks and sometimes such features as anti-lock brakes and automatic transmissions. As there are well over a dozen specialist chassis makers in America alone we have included a small representative selection. Many make chassis that ultimately carry only the name of the body-work and equipment manufacturer and many also have the same style of Cincinatti steel cab. Along with the roadgoing fire appliance we show some examples of the special all-wheel drive rapid intervention and crash tender vehicles for aircraft accidents.

In this section we also feature some highway maintenance vehicles such as snow ploughs, and look at some different types of refuse collectors. The latter are, of course, often mounted on regular truck chassis with minor modifications, so we are limiting coverage here to specialist models.

Shelvoke Dempster of Letchworth, England, makes this ultra-narrow PN Revopak refuse collector which shreds and compresses household refuse. It has a Perkins diesel and a steel and fibreglass tilt cab.

Shelvoke Dempster **RouteChief 623** has the American designed Dempster rear loading system. This example holds 30 cu. yds. which can be compressed to a legal highway payload of 12·8 tonnes within its 24·39 tonnes GVW. It has a Leyland 180 bhp diesel with Eaton manual or Allison automatic transmission.

Shelvoke Dempster **SPV** fire appliance chassis with Angloco bodywork. Various engines by Perkins, Leyland and others are available in the 180 to 230 bhp range with manual or automatic transmission.

158

Oshkosh make this **P-2527** snow plough and gritter 4 × 4 chassis. Cummins 300 or 350 bhp diesels drive Fuller or Allison gearboxes and Oshkosh front and Rockwell rear axles.

Oshkosh **DA-1500** in an 8 × 8 pivot-steer high mobility crash, fire and rescue vehicle. It has a Detroit 540 bhp diesel with Allison automatic transmission. It can accelerate from 0–50 mph (80 kph) in 40 seconds and can climb a 60 per cent gradient. The 5460 litres per minute pump has a Detroit 300 bhp diesel.

Federal Motors makes this 4 × 4 chassis for fire and utility applications. It is an **FT44** model with Deutz V-8 air-cooled diesel. Similar chassis are manufactured by Pemfab of Racocas, New Jersey.

Faun makes such municipal equipment as gulley empti-ers, refuse collectors and street sweepers. This is their **AK3320HB** sweeper which has a 7·5 tonne GVW, an 80 bhp diesel and a 700 litre water tank for its sprinklers.

An example of a Russian ZIL 6 × 6 fire appliance in Bulgaria. It is a **13L AC-40** model. Note the tyre pressure adjusters. In Bulgaria Liaz and GAZ trucks are built under licence, the latter with Perkins diesels in place of their more usual Russian petrol units.

This French refuse collector might at first appear to be on a Renault diesel chassis. However, though some Renault components are used, the **Sita 5102** is in fact an electrically propelled vehicle.

American LaFrance offer two- and three-axle refuse collectors as well as fire appliances. This low cab model is suitable for front-loading bin equipment. It has a Caterpillar eight-cylinder diesel (with Cummins and Detroit options) and Allison automatic transmission.

Reynolds Boughton of Winkleigh, Devon, England, make chassis for numerous fire equipment makers. This is a 525 bhp Mercedes-Benz engined Centaurus chassis used by Rosenbauer of Linz, Austria as the basis for their Simba crash tender. It has Allison transmission, 6 × 6 with Kirkstall axles and a GVW of 28 tonnes. Similar chassis are also made for Rosenbauer by Titan in West Germany.

Fresia of Millesimo, Italy, specializes in snow ploughs and 4 × 4 chassis to propel them. Many of their models are convertible into normal tippers for summer use. This **F90L** has a Fiat 130 bhp diesel and steering on both axles. The snow blades are powered by a 260 bhp Fiat diesel, though 480 bhp can also be specified.

This Sides-equipped Faun 8 × 8 airport crash tender has twin Deutz V-12 air cooled 500 bhp diesels with ZF torque converter transmission. It can accelerate to 80 kph in 37 seconds at 50 tonnes GVW (including 18,000 litres of water). The monitor has a range of 70 metres.

Hendrickson of Lyons, Illinois, makes chassis for various fire appliance manufacturers. This is its **1871-W** low profile truck with six-seat steel or aluminium cab and choice of engines up to a 445 bhp diesel. 4 × 2, 4 × 4, 6 × 4 and 6 × 6 types are produced.

RFW fire proof Australian bushfire truck carries 5,000 litres of water and 500 litres of chemicals. It has 4 × 4, Allison transmission and a 250 bhp Caterpillar diesel.

Terberg makes a number of narrow (two metres wide) chassis for municipal use. This is their DAF 6·17 litre diesel powered **TSR 1000.** It is also available with a Volvo engine for refuse collection. Another version is built for street sweeping with four-wheel steering.

Made in both Canada and the USA by the old established Walter firm are 4 × 4 crash tender chassis and snow ploughs. They feature automatic locking, torque proportioning differentials for positive traction. This Snow Fighter with hinge-out vee blade can have various engine options up to about 400 bhp.

Walter airport crash trucks have the same four-point positive drive as Snow Fighters with hub reduction gearing and special differentials. They can have diesels of up to 540 bhp.

As well as building fire trucks on other brands of chassis, Sides of Saint Nazaire. France, make complete crash tenders. The **S2.000** has a water capacity of 15,200 or 11,000 litres and a 90 metre monitor range. It has 6 × 6 and a 780 bhp diesel.

Oshkosh **H-2318** has a 205 bhp Detroit driving its 4 × 4 chassis and a 492 bhp Detroit powering the rotary snow plough. It has Allison automatic transmission and option of rear wheel steering.

Oshkosh build this **P-15** for the US Air Force. It has separate 492 bhp Detroit diesels driving each tandem and twin Allison torque converter transmissions. Total weight with 28,200 litres of water and 2,300 litres of chemicals is 65 tons and 0–50 mph (80 kph) acceleration takes 48 seconds.

Oshkosh **P-19** rapid intervention vehicle has a 400 bhp
Cummins diesel with Allison automatic transmission. 0–
50 mph (80 kph) acceleration takes 25 seconds. GVW
is 15·24 tonnes.

Oshkosh **T-1500** reaches 50 mph (80 kph) in 25
seconds thanks to a rear-mounted Detroit 540 bhp
diesel and Allison transmission. GVW is 20·7 tonnes.
Top speed is 65 mph (105 kph) with 6,825 litres water
and 900 litres chemicals.

Spartan fire appliance chassis made in Charlotte, Michigan, with Spacemaster steel cab. It has a Detroit 239 bhp diesel with Spicer five-speed gearbox. Two- and three-axle versions are offered.

Spartan **CFC-2000** has five-man steel cab and diesels of up to 492 bhp with five- or six-speed manual or automatic transmissions. 6 × 4 and 6 × 6 versions are also built. Pemfab, Federal, Hendrickson, Pirsch, Duplex, Hahn, Pierce and Sutphen are some of the other builders of American custom fire chassis.

This is Mack's **CF Pumper** with choice of Mack Diesels of 237 to 350 bhp. Mack, like Magirus in the IVECO group, is unusual for being a major truck producer that also retains a special department building fire appliances. Another example is the Scammell special vehicle division of Leyland, which makes Nubian crash tender chassis.

Dennis of Guildford, England, makes various complete municipal vehicles and fire appliances. They typically have Perkins or Rolls-Royce engines and manual or Allison transmission.

This Hendrickson **1879** chassis is relatively unusual for having 4 × 4. It has been equipped for fire fighting by Emergency One and has a 6,825 litres per minute pump. The 1879 can have various engines, Detroit often being specified, and has a tilt-cab.

FTF occasionally makes chassis for fire equipment. This pair of Detroit-powered trucks carry a hydraulic platform with pump on the 8 × 4 and a foam monitor and pump on the 6 × 4.

Meili of Schubelbach, Switzerland, makes various 4 × 4 trucks and also markets the Italian **Sirmac** on which this Rampini fire fighting equipment is mounted. The 4 × 4 chassis has Ford or Fiat engines of up to 216 bhp.

The former Thornycroft Nubian fire crash tenders are now made by Scammell and have been redesigned with rear mounted Cummins diesels and 6 × 6 or 4 × 4, as shown on this chassis with test weight.

A Reynolds Boughton 6 × 6 crash tender is shown earlier and this is its 4 × 4 **Pegasus,** equipped with Chubb Spearhead equipment, undergoing a tilt test. It has a 235 bhp Rolls-Royce petrol engine and Allison gearbox. Top speed is 62 mph (100 kph) and 50 mph (80 kph) can be reached in 25 seconds.

Magirus-Deutz, or Magirus as it is now known in the IVECO group, makes all manner of fire equipment. This 310 bhp 6 × 4 chassis carries a Magirus 30-metre turntable ladder.

Heavy Haulage

Several of the earlier sections contained massive vehicles. Notably they were the trucks used off normal highways that therefore had no legal constraints on their size. Classic examples were the heavy dump trucks, which may spend all their lives within a mile or two's radius of a pit and are limited in size only by cost and availability of tyres and other components. In this final part of the book we look at an assortment of vehicles used to haul indivisible loads on highways and in yards and factories around the world. As well as the products of the specialist makers, ultra heavy duty tractors are also offered by several of the major multinationals (Volvo-White, Leyland/Scammell, PACCAR, Mercedes-Benz, Scania, MAN/ÖAF, IVECO, Renault/Mack, etc.).

Titan in West Germany makes various heavy tractors often based on Mercedes-Benz components. A 6 × 6 type is shown under *Off-highway* and here we have one of their traction heads that can be directly coupled to many types of semi-trailers.

Faun of Lauf a.d. Pegnitz, West Germany, makes an extensive range of heavy haulage tractive units for GTW of up to 400 tonnes with 4 × 4, 6 × 6, 8 × 6 or 8 × 8, and Deutz, Cummins or Detroit diesels of up to 780 bhp. This forward control 6 × 6 unit employs an IVECO cab.

8 × 8 Faun tractors have Detroit 780 bhp diesels with Allison transmission for 400 tonnes GTW and Deutz or Cummins 525–575 bhp diesels with manual or automatic transmission for 300 tonnes GTW.

The Titan 6 × 6 **Z4042/Z4052** has 420 or 525 bhp Mercedes-Benz diesels and ZF Transmatic gearbox. GTW is 200 tonnes. A broadly similar machine is now also offered by Mercedes-Benz itself.

Titan industrial tractor and trailer is for 150 or 200 tonne loads and is powered by Mercedes-Benz 168 or 256 bhp diesel with ZF gearboxes. These tractors are used primarily in shipyards and foundries.

Faun **HZ 36.40/45** is a 6 × 6 tractor with 365 bhp Deutz diesel and Fuller gearbox. It is for 180 tonnes GTW. Mercedes-Benz or Cummins diesels can also be specified.

Pacific of North Vancouver has supplied 18 heavy tractors to South Africa Railways. The largest have 750 bhp diesels and can be used in multiples for ultra heavy loads.

Pacific, logging trucks are used in Canada, Australia,
New Zealand, Indonesia, Malaysia and the Philippines.
They can have Detroit, Cummins or Caterpillar diesels
in the 300 to 500 bhp range and Allison, Fuller or Spicer
gearboxes. Many have 1825 litre water tanks for brake
cooling on long downgrades.

Terberg build heavy haulage units employing such
Volvo units as cab, eight-speed synchro gearbox with
optional splitter for 16 ratios, and engine. This **F1450**
6 × 4 has a 308 bhp diesel and axles by Rockwell.

Kaelble of Backnang, West Germany, makes this **K4VW615Z.** It has a MAN V-12 turbo 615 bhp diesel with Allison six-speed power shift transmission, Kaeble transfer box and four Kessler hub reduction axles. The engine is behind the cab and with ballast the tractor weighs 45 tonnes and has GTW of 500 tonnes.

Kaelble **KD34S330** has a Mercedes-Benz V-8 14·62 litre, 330 bhp diesel and eight-speed ZF synchro gearbox. The maximum fifth wheel load is 28 tonnes for up to 135 tonnes GTW and GVW is 39·3 tonnes.

179

Kaelble **KDV 24Z 420** is a 6 × 6 tractor with Mercedes-Benz 420 bhp diesel and ZF gearbox. GTW is 185 tonnes. A Deutz air-cooled turbo diesel can be alternatively specified.

Kaelble **KVW 320 IZ** is an industrial tractor for foundries and shipyards. It has a Mercedes-Benz 320 bhp diesel, ZF gearbox and 4 × 4. Loads of up to 180 tonnes can be towed.

Faun makes molten metal and hot slag transporters for foundries. These can lift and carry up to 90 tonnes at a time and have 198 to 300 bhp diesels.

Scammell is covered under Leyland in the *Major Groups* section, but no look at heavy haulage is complete without an example of their vehicles. This is an **S26** normal control outfit with T45 tilt cab and Cummins 350 bhp diesel. GCW is 65 tonnes, though bonneted models are available for GTW of 200 plus tonnes.

Hendrickson has built 6 × 6 tractors for GTW of over 500 tons. Various engines are available including Detroit diesels of up to 635 bhp.

Hendrickson tank retriever can carry 60 tons at up to 62 mph. It has a 45 tons capacity winch. An associated Hendrickson company makes tandem axle suspension units employed by many makers of heavy trucks.

The Belgian MOL firm acquired the rights to build French PRP-Willème heavy tractors and this is the resulting **TG250** 8 × 8. It is for 250 tonnes GTW and has a Cummins 450 bhp six-cylinder turbo diesel and Clark torque converter/gearbox with Kessler hub reduction axles.

MOL **T5264/05** 6 × 4 is for 150 tonnes GTW and has a Cummins 400 bhp diesel and Fuller 15-speed gearbox. It has Kessler hub reduction rear axles.

Oshkosh **M-911** is for 109 tonnes GTW and has a
Detroit 435 bhp V-8 two-stroke diesel with Allison
automatic torque converter transmission. All the axles
are driven except for the air suspended one in the middle
which can be lowered to reduce loading on the other
axles by up to nine tonnes.

The French trailer-maker Nicolas of Champs sur Yonne
has introduced self-propelled load carriers and tractors
in recent years. This is a pair of Automas modular units
with hydrostatic wheel motors and 150 tonnes capacity.
The wheels are shown in their sideways travelling position.

An Automas 140 tonne capacity carrier for hot steel slabs. The knee-action wheel supports can be lowered hydraulically and the truck then driven out from under its load and landing legs.

Front view of an Automas unit. The largest can carry 540 tonnes (or more with additional units added). The hydrostatic wheel motors are driven by diesel engines underneath the platform.

Nicolas Tractomas is available with 6 × 4, 6 × 6, 8 × 4 or 8 × 8. All feature a Renault cab and engines by Detroit, Mercedes-Benz, and Cummins of 430 to 810 bhp. Axles are mostly by Soma and transmissions by Clark, Fuller, ZF or Allison. GVW is up to 74 tonnes and GTW to 400 tonnes.

Lyka of Preston, England, formed by an ex-Atkinson employee, has made trailer spotters since 1974 and has recently added heavy trucks to the range. They include bonneted 6 × 6 450 bhp 100 tonne tractors and this 70 tonne GVW steel carrier with Rolls-Royce 220 bhp diesel and Spicer gearbox.

The FTF **FS-10.30DSS** 8 × 4 is for 40 tonnes GVW and has Allison or Fuller transmission and a Detroit 414 bhp V-8 diesel. It has front and rear steering axles though an 8 × 4 with twin steering front axles is also available.

FTF makes 6 × 4 chassis for heavy load carrying or as tractive units, with 324 or 414 bhp Detroit diesels and Motor Panels cabs. This example has a ballast box and cab-guard for use in confined factory areas.

Camb of Nonantola, Italy, makes unusual rigid low-loaders with triple rear axles and one or two steered front axles. Here one carries a 42·1 tonne earthmover. The Camb has a Fiat 11·5 litre diesel and eight-speed gearbox.

Cometto of Cuneo, Italy, is well-known as a trailer maker but it also builds powered modules of many types and sizes. Its standard 6, 8 and 10 axle modules carry respectively 110, 150 and 190 tonnes. Scheurle makes similar machines in Germany.

Irtex is a small French manufacturer of heavy haulage vehicles with René Harvey (the Willème designer—see MOL) as their chief engineer. This 60 tonne GVW 8 × 8 has Mercedes-Benz 430 bhp diesel, ZF gearbox, Soma axles and DAF cab. Versions are also sold by TMU of Bilbao (see *Off-highway* section).

Tracked heavy transport modules are made by Manitowoc in the USA. This pair are shown with a 1,050 ton load. Each is powered by two 375 bhp Caterpillar diesels driving through torque converters. The tracks help to reduce ground pressure.

Kamag of Ulm, West Germany, built this 700 tonne capacity carrier. It has 160 electronically controlled wheels, 32 of which are driven. There are two man cabs at each end and the outfit is 23 metres long.

ÖAF in Austria build most of MAN's heavy haulage units. This is a **40.400DFAS** with 6 × 6 and a 400 bhp MAN V-10 turbo diesel. It has a ZF Transmatic gearbox and is designed for 250 tonnes GTW.

INDEX OF TRUCK MAKERS